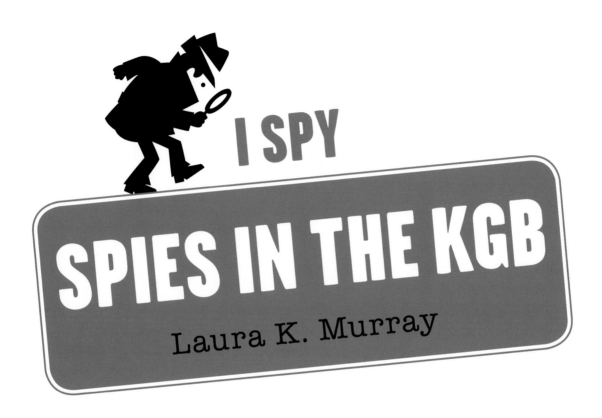

I SPY

SPIES IN THE KGB

Laura K. Murray

Creative Education ⊕ Creative Paperbacks

Published by Creative Education and Creative Paperbacks
P.O. Box 227, Mankato, Minnesota 56002
Creative Education and Creative Paperbacks
are imprints of **The Creative Company**
www.thecreativecompany.us

Design and production by **Christine Vanderbeek**
Art direction by **Rita Marshall**
Printed in the **United States of America**

Photographs by Alamy (Mihail Chekalov, Ian Shaw), Corbis
(Bettmann, Hulton-Deutsch Collection, LUKE MACGREGOR/
Reuters), Dreamstime (Stuart Monk), Getty Images
(Jeffrey Coolidge, FBI, Sasha Mordovets), Shutterstock
(Alexandr III, BeRad, Milos Djapovic, M. Shcherbyna,
SoRad, tele52)

Library of Congress Cataloging-in-Publication Data
Murray, Laura K.
Spies in the KGB / Laura K. Murray.
p. cm. — (I spy)
Includes index.
Summary: An early reader's guide to KGB spies, introduc-
ing Russian espionage history, famous agents such as Oleg
Penkovsky, techniques such as dead drops, and the dangers
all spies face.
ISBN 978-1-60818-617-4 (hardcover)
ISBN 978-1-62832-229-3 (pbk)
ISBN 978-1-56660-664-6 (eBook)
1. Espionage, Soviet—Juvenile literature. 2. Espionage,
Russian—Juvenile literature. 3. Spies—Soviet Union—
Juvenile literature. 4. Spies—Russia (Federation)—Juvenile
literature. I. Title.

UB271.R9M87 2015
327.1247—dc23   2014048719

CCSS: RI.1.1, 2, 3, 4, 5, 6, 7, 10; RI.2.1, 2, 3, 5, 6, 7; RI.3.1,
3, 5, 7; RF.1.1, 3, 4; RF.2.4

First Edition HC 9 8 7 6 5 4 3 2 1
First Edition PBK 9 8 7 6 5 4 3 2 1

TABLE OF CONTENTS

I SPY

A RUSSIAN SPY SITS IN A

busy train station. He looks
left and right. Then he sticks a
computer disk under his seat.
It is a **dead drop**! The spy gets
on a train and disappears.

Russian leader Vladimir
Putin was a KGB spy.

Russia

SPIES WORK ALL OVER THE

world. They work in secret to gather information. Russian spies used to work for the KGB. Today, many work for the SVR.

RUSSIA HAS USED SPIES

for years. Klaus Fuchs (*FOOKS*) stole secrets about American bombs. Later, **Cold War** spies worked inside the United States.

COOL SPIES

Wimbledon special
Can Andy Murray tame the Beast?
SPORT S1-7 PLUS LAURA ROBSON PUPPY FAT ROW PAGE 7

Jamie O
How he w
over school
ROSE PRINCE COMMENT PAGE 25

The Daily Telegraph

NEWSPAPER OF THE YEAR

Friday, July 2, 2010

Irish Republic €1.20

The spy who loved m

- **MI5 call came as little surprise, says ex-husband**

- Her KGB father cont her life, he a

EXCLUSIVE

By Andy Bloxham and Gordon Rayner

MI5 is investigating whether a former KGB agent recruited his daughter to work for the country's secret services while living in London.

Anna Chapman told her British ex-husband that her father, Vasily Kushchenko, was a "high ranking" officer in the country's security forces, *The Daily Telegraph* can disclose.

On Wednesday an MI5 officer interviewed Alex Chapman at his home in Bournemouth as part of the Security Service's investigation into the background of Mrs Chapman, 28, who has been accused of spying in the US.

MI5 is trying to discover

their honeymoon in 2002 in Zimbabwe, where he was serving as a diplomat.

"I asked her what her father's job was and Anna just said he was there to represent the Russian government in certain areas of government." said Mr Chapman. "He didn't trust anyone. He asked me why I had chosen a Russian bride and asked what business I had in Russia, and I said none.

"He was scary. He would

INSIDE

It was love at first sight, but Anna changed
Reports: Pages 2-3

Anna Chapman is devoted to

ness ban
Barclays a
a hedge
gator Asse
is thought
whether
accounts o
als, and w
be any se
for Britain.

She late
internet e
after going
2006 whe
ended, mov
2007 where
another onl
ture. Mr Ch
ex-wife had
Americans, c
their accent,
denly in 200
desperate to g
"business opp
He said: "
rich Americar

Dear Mr Rascal
Exclusive: the Prince Charles correspondence
VIEWSPAPER PAGE 4

SECRETS AND LIES

RUSSIAN *AGENTS* **LEARN** many languages. They try to blend in. Sometimes they have to lie about their job.

RUSSIAN SPIES GO TO A

special school. It is in
Moscow. The training lasts
for two or more years.

U.S. agents called
Penkovsky by his
secret name, "Hero."

OLEG PENKOVSKY WAS A KGB

spy. He became a **double agent**
for the U.S. He gave secrets
about Russian weapons.

STAR AGENT

HIDDEN TOOLS

woven wick, and
roken pieces of the trestle
facedown in the center of

ldn't just leave her there
was found like this. He
e this.
uld enjoy listening to
ell him all the maca-
ed. The very idea of
ut in such a grisly
to know who had
eople everywhere
d gruesome end,

fe, where he'd
y lamp on the
Couldn't have
said it a lot.

it into the
he quilted
t it razor
nd slop
untold
up of
d eat

wealthy? Some of that money, earned by his mother from her spinning

A RUSSIAN SPY COULD BE

hiding anything. A tube of
lipstick might be a gun. A shoe
could be a radio! A spy uses
bugs to hear people talking.

CATCHING A SPY

SPIES DO NOT WANT TO GET

caught. American Robert Hanssen
sold secrets to the KGB. He got
away with it for 22 years! He was
finally arrested in 2001.

SOME RUSSIAN SPIES ARE

very tricky. They share fake secrets. Then enemy spies get all mixed up! Agents get paid. New orders tell them where to go next.

NEVER DONE

TOP SECRET

they
s rece
n cov

TOP-SECRET ACTIVITY

#1276: Make a Dead Drop

Spies use dead drops to pass secrets to one another without getting caught. Make your own dead drop with a fellow spy!

Tools:

secret message
  or object
rubber band
  or piece of yarn

Orders: Look around for a good place to hide objects or messages. It could be under a bed or behind a tree. Hide your message at the dead drop. Then put a rubber band or piece of yarn on a doorknob. That will show the other spy that a message is waiting!

Why do you think it is important for spies to keep secrets?

GLOSSARY

agents   people who work as spies

bugs   hidden objects used for listening in secret

Cold War   the time from 1947 to 1991 when Russia and the U.S. spied on each other and were in danger of going to war

dead drop   a secret spot where a spy can leave objects or messages for another spy to pick up

double agent   a spy who pretends to work for one country while really working for another

READ MORE

Stewart, James. *Spies and Traitors*. North Mankato, Minn.: Smart Apple Media, 2008.

Walker, Kate, and Elaine Argaet. *So You Want to Be a Spy*. North Mankato, Minn.: Smart Apple Media, 2004.

WEBSITES

INTERNATIONAL SPY MUSEUM: KIDSPY ZONE

http://www.spymuseum.org /education-programs/kids-families /kidspy-zone/
Play spy games, and learn how to talk like a secret agent.

NICK JR.: HARRIET THE SPY

http://www.nick.com/games/spy -test-with-harriet-the-spy.html
Test your spy skills with the help of Harriet the Spy.

Note: Every effort has been made to ensure that the websites listed above are suitable for children, that they have educational value, and that they contain no inappropriate material. However, because of the nature of the Internet, it is impossible to guarantee that these sites will remain active indefinitely or that their contents will not be altered.

INDEX